R.I.S.E.

R.I.S.E.

Reflections That Shape Who You Become

Ricardo León

Published by Casa León Press

ISBN: 979-8-9950431-0-2 (Paperback)

First Edition: 2026

ricardoleon.net

hello@ricardoleon.net

For my mom, who taught me strength by how she lived
and love by how she gave.
I miss you.

For my wife, Jesy, and my son, Sebastian.
Thank you for your love, your patience, and for growing
with me through the tough times.

For my brother, who faces Parkinson's with a strength
most will never understand.
I see you, and I love you.

CONTENTS

INTRODUCTION

I grew up poor.

My mom worked hard.

Two jobs, no complaints, just kept moving.

I didn't grow up with a lot, but I grew up watching someone who never waited for perfect conditions.

For most of my life, I've had a positive, go-for-it attitude.

But that didn't happen by accident.

Around fifteen years old, I picked up two books that changed how I thought about myself and what was possible: *Unlimited Power by Tony Robbins* and *The 7 Habits of Highly Effective People by Stephen Covey*.

I've been studying self-development for over thirty-five years.

Even after all the books, training, certifications, and workshops, I still catch myself thinking:
"I could do better."
"Why are they more successful than me?"
"What am I doing wrong?"

I've always known I'm capable of great things.

But knowing you're capable is not the same as acting like it.

This book doesn't exist because I have it all figured out, but because I keep choosing to work at it.

Nothing New

Let me be upfront about something: there is nothing groundbreaking in self-development.

It's like saying, "This is a new antique."

It doesn't exist.

The principles work.

They always have.

What changes lives isn't a new idea.

It's the right reminder at the right moment.

That's why this book works for anyone.

For beginners who have never read a personal development book, this is where you begin.

For the one who's read everything, you'll find things in here you already know.

That's intentional.

Because knowing something and living it are two different things.

People aren't stuck because they lack new information.

They're stuck because they forget what they already know.

Already on the Path

I've read and worked through several frameworks over the years.

Some of them were excellent.

But almost every one assumed I was starting at zero.

What if you're already on your path and just need a reminder, some clarity, or a fresh perspective?

That's who this book is for too.

If you're struggling with how you communicate, go to Influence.

If you're running on empty, start with Energy.

If you can't get honest with yourself, go to Self-Awareness.

If you keep getting in your own way, go to Self-Accountability.

If you're waiting for the right conditions to move, go to Resourcefulness.

There's no wrong door.

Why Decisions, Not Habits or Goals

Habits do not determine identity.

They reveal it.

Goals don't hold under pressure.

When difficulty arrives, goals become negotiable. Identity does not.

This book is about decisions.

Not those dramatic, one-time declarations but the quiet, internal commitments that determine how you act, regardless of circumstances.

Here is the difference.

A habit: What should I do?

A goal: What should I achieve?

A decision: Who am I committed to being?

When you are clear about who you are committed to being, the behavior takes care of itself.

When you're unclear, no amount of willpower or motivation will be enough.

The shifts that made a difference in my life did not come from better tactics or bigger goals.

I had to get clear on what I wanted.

Then decide who I was committed to being to get there.

You either make the decision or the decision gets made for you.

What Is R.I.S.E.

Everything I've studied in mindset, leadership, and personal growth comes down to four areas: R.I.S.E.

I've been teaching it as the core of my coaching and training practice for over six years.

Resourcefulness: The decision to use what you have instead of waiting for what you do not.

Influence: The decision to manage your state so you lift the people around you instead of draining them.

Self-Awareness: The decision to tell yourself the truth without judgment so you can choose differently.

Energy: The decision to protect what fuels you and stop giving your best to the things that deserve your least.

Running through all four is **Self-Accountability,** the willingness to ask honestly:
What is my part in this?

How to Use This Book

This is a book of reflections.

Each section gives you principles and a question.

One reflection a day works.

So does reading a full section at once.

When a question lands, answer it.

Not in your head.

On paper.

One honest sentence written down is worth more than an hour of thinking about it.

Pick a reflection.

Answer the question.

Decide.

Then do it.

R

RESOURCEFULNESS

Resourcefulness is the first decision in R.I.S.E. for a reason.

Without it, nothing else works.

Resourcefulness isn't about having more money, time, connections, or skills.

It's about using what you already have.

Every experience, every lesson, every relationship.

We forget to use them.

We go looking for the next new thing instead of drawing on what we already have.

You've had times where everything looked right on paper, and you still felt stuck.

And times where life was falling apart, and somehow you figured it out.

The difference was never the circumstances.

It was the decision to use what you already had.

Being resourceful means getting out of your own way.

When you hit a wall, that's exactly when you tap into it.

Resourcefulness is the ability to tap into something different when you need it most.

This section is about one decision.

Stop waiting and use what's already in front of you.

The decision:

Use what you have instead of waiting for what you don't. The resource you're looking for is closer than you think.

Inner vs. Outer Resources

There are two kinds of resources you can tap into.

Outer resources are tools around you: time, money,
people, and skills.

Inner resources are what you carry: belief, grit, adaptability, and follow-through.

Inner resources and outer resources work together.

Inner resourcefulness without outer resources has limits.

Outer resources without inner resourcefulness leave you waiting.

Develop and use both.

PERSPECTIVE

Your lens determines your options.

Difficulty teaches.

This isn't positive thinking.

It's noticing what life is trying to show you.

Every limitation forces a new path.

Every obstacle forces you to look somewhere you weren't looking.

When I lost jobs, when plans fell apart, the opportunity wasn't obvious at the time.

Looking back, the difficulty was always teaching me something I needed.

You have to stay engaged long enough to see it.

What is this current difficulty trying to teach me?

Constraints create clarity.

This sounds like a catchphrase.

When I moved to Dallas without a guaranteed job, the obstacle was real: no safety net, no backup plan.

That constraint forced clarity.

I knew what I wanted, and the lack of options made me sharper, more decisive, more willing to bet on myself.

Constraints don't limit resourceful people.

They focus them.

Which constraint could sharpen my focus right now?

Perspective creates options.

Pausing under pressure gives you options.

The option to choose a different perspective, emotional state, or strategy.

Change how you see the situation so new resources become available.

That's the shift.

The perspective that got you stuck won't get you out.

Step outside the perspective that created the problem.

How would this challenge look from a completely different angle?

Better questions, better outcomes.

Resourceful and unresourceful people look at the same situation and ask different questions.

One asks, "Why is this happening to me?"

The other asks, "Who or what can help me solve this faster?"

Same situation.

Completely different answers and outcomes.

The questions you ask shape the resources you find.

Am I asking questions that move me forward?

The unconventional fix.

When working on an IT issue or a mindset issue, there are thousands of ways to solve a problem you've never seen before.

You don't always have the textbook answer.

Sometimes the obvious solution doesn't work.

That's when resourcefulness kicks in.

You start looking for the unconventional fix.

The workaround nobody tried.

The clever path nobody thought to take.

Looking for the unconventional fix isn't a personality trait.

It's what happens when you refuse to give up on finding a way.

Where's the option I'm not letting myself see?

MOMENTUM

Movement creates opportunity.

Choose before life forces you.

My mom worked two jobs.

She came home exhausted, body aching, and got up the next day to do it again.

Necessity made her the most resourceful person I've ever known.

When you have no choice, you figure it out.

Every time you put it off, the limiting story that you can't gets a little stronger.

The cost doesn't hit you all at once.

It creeps up on you.

One day you wake up and realize you've become someone you didn't consciously choose to be.

Not through failure, but through a thousand small surrenders.

What decision can I make now before pressure makes it for me?

Fear hides your next move.

One of my favorite quotes comes from Eleanor Roosevelt.
She asked, "What could we accomplish if we knew we couldn't fail?"

It exposes how often fear runs the show.

Most of the excuses I hear:
"I'm not ready,"
"It's not the right time,"
"I need more information."

That's BS to avoid doing what you know you have to do.

Strip away the fear, and you already know exactly what you'd do.

The resource isn't missing.

The courage to use it is.

If failure wasn't possible, what would I do today?

Start before you're ready.

Action is the antidote to overthinking.

You don't need more time.

You don't need better conditions.

You don't need to feel ready.

Twenty-five years in IT, and I never really felt ready for what came next.

There was always a new role, a new system, and a new problem.

I just had to figure it out on the way.

You get ready by moving and doing something, not by expecting to feel it.

What can I begin today before I feel fully ready?

Keep moving.

After my mom passed, I slowed down, almost stopped altogether.

My energy was depleted.

My patience was short.

I pulled back from everything I could.

But I didn't stop.

I rescheduled my mastermind and training event once, then made myself run it.
I almost canceled my annual nonprofit event, Baskets For Good, but pushed through and did it in her honor.

I didn't feel like it, but I kept a speaking engagement and still added value.

Refuse to quit when quitting would be easier.

Do I give myself credit for moving when stopping would be easier?

STANDARDS

How you respond is the resource.

Composure is contagious.

Composure and confidence under pressure are resources people forget they have.

During major system outages, I learned that my calm confidence was more valuable than my technical skills.

If I panicked, the whole room escalated.

If I stayed composed, people trusted that the situation was being handled.

How you respond determines everything that follows.

When I am under pressure, do I keep my composure, or do I let the obstacle control my response?

Run your day.

A client once told me they didn't have time to work out.

We didn't try to find more time.

We dug into where their attention was going.

They were spending hours reacting to emails, messages, interruptions, and calling it productivity.

The missing resource wasn't time; it was priority.

When they made health the priority, it got done.

Within three months, they were healthier and in control of their day.

Where have I lowered my standard and let interruptions replace intention?

Through is the way.

There's no shortcut through grief, through growth, through the hard times and conversations you've been avoiding.

I know because I've tried every detour.

After losing my mom, I wanted to go around the pain, avoid it at all costs.

But the only way my energy returned was by going through it, doing what I had to do, and letting myself feel the grief while still moving forward.

I didn't feel like doing any of it.

But it had to be done, so I did it.

Through is the only direction that leads somewhere real.

What am I trying to go around that I must go through?

Problems give direction.

Problems are signals to engage.

I have had moments when a problem surfaced and demanded everything I had.

Sometimes we back away when we should be diving in.

A problem doesn't have to stop you.

It can focus you.

The harder the problem, the more locked in you become.

What problem is asking me to lock in, rather than back away?

Change is a standard.

Knowing you need to change and changing are two completely different things.

I've been stuck.

I knew I was stuck.

And I still stayed there longer than I should have.

High standards don't mean you always get it right.

They mean you refuse to keep doing what isn't working.

You don't need all the answers.

You must be willing to let go of what isn't working.

Where am I tolerating less than my own standard?

Break the pattern.

The same thoughts.

The same reactions.

The same strategies.

They keep you running in circles, hoping this will eventually produce a different result.

It never does.

You have to break the pattern.

Ask a different question.

Try a different approach.

Call someone you wouldn't normally call.

The pattern is the problem.

Breaking it is the resource.

Am I expecting a different result from the same mindset?

BUILD

Build from where you are.

Build the door.

I walked into my first IT interview in shorts and a t-shirt.

I didn't have a high school diploma or a college degree.

I didn't know Excel.

I didn't know Windows.

I'd never touched a computer.

But I said yes when I was asked.

That afternoon, I bought the books and taught myself everything I'd claimed to know.

That wasn't luck.

That was building my own door.

What door could I build today instead of waiting for one to open?

Something new.

When you spend all your energy fighting what's not working, you have nothing left to build what could.

I've watched people exhaust themselves trying to fix broken situations.

The resourceful move?

Redirect and build.

Stop pouring energy into something that's already done and start investing in what's next.

Where am I fighting the old when I should be building the new?

Nothing is wasted.

It's not about controlling circumstances.

It's about adjusting your response.

I've been laid off.

I've walked away from roles.

I've had plans fall apart.

The fact is: Something is always going to fall apart.

Stop fighting what's already done.

Start building with what's still there.

What have I written off that I could still build with?

Use what shaped you.

YES! Anything!

The good, the bad, and the ugly.

Your setbacks, your failures, your pain, they are all resources waiting to be used.

My background, my losses, my mother's death, the jobs that didn't work out, none of that was wasted.

Everything I've experienced has shaped how I lead and teach.

Tap into your experience, and if that's not enough, ask for help.

What setback am I refusing to learn from?

Innovate.

Resourceful people don't just work harder.

They look for a better way.

They borrow ideas, combine them, and make something better and more effective.

I've done this my entire career.

Taking a process, an idea, finding the gap, and making it better.

It's about refusing to accept that the current way is the best way.

The status quo is just the starting point.

Where is the status quo costing me?

Resourcefulness beats resources.

I've known people with every advantage who went nowhere, and people with almost nothing who figured it out.

The difference was never what resources they had.

It was whether they decided to use them.

Resourcefulness isn't a trait you're born with; it's a switch.

You either flip it, or you don't.

What resource am I sitting on right now that I haven't used?

I

INFLUENCE

Influence isn't something you turn on when you need it.

It's always on.

Every room you walk into responds to your presence, energy, and tone.

People feel it before you say a word.

Influence is heart-centered leadership.

It's the ability to bring out the best in the people around you.

Sometimes it happens naturally, and sometimes you have to work at it.

But it's always there.

Real influence makes people feel seen, valued, and capable of more.

That's what separates leaders people tolerate from leaders people remember.

You're influencing someone every day.

At work, at home, in your marriage, with your kids, with your team.

The only question is whether you're doing it intentionally or by default.

The decision:

Manage your state so you lift the people around you instead of draining them.

PRESENCE

Your state sets the tone.

Your state leads.

You can say all the right things and still drain a room.

I've done it.

Overwhelmed, tired, and doing too much, I brought tension into every interaction without realizing it.

It wasn't what I was saying.

It was the energy I was projecting.

But when I'm present, grounded, and intentional, the whole atmosphere shifts.

People aren't influenced by what you say first.

They are influenced by the energy you carry.

What am I bringing into the room before I say a word?

Beyond the title.

During a major outage, leadership is asking questions; they want answers now.

I didn't add to that energy.

When I joined the all-hands conference call, the first thing I said was, "Give me a few minutes to assess the situation."

That became my way to reset the room.

When I stayed composed, people trusted that the situation was being handled.

I didn't need authority or a title to influence.

Where in my life do I have more influence than I realize?

Two kinds of influence.

Before you can lead a room, you have to lead yourself.

The way you manage your thoughts, emotions, and responses under pressure is internal influence.

What it produces in the people around you, the tone, the trust, the standard, that's external influence.

I've watched leaders with real authority lose a room because they couldn't manage what was happening inside them.

The room felt it before a word was said.

You can't separate the two.

How you lead yourself defines how you lead others.

Where is my internal state affecting the people around me right now?

Authority without influence.

I've been in rooms where someone leaned hard on their title instead of their presence.

"Because I said so."

"This is coming from above."

Nothing killed my motivation faster.

Authority can force behavior, but it can't inspire commitment.

The people who influenced me most never pulled rank.

They were consistent, listened before speaking, and earned respect through action.

None of it came from their title.

What kind of leader am I when nobody is required to follow me?

Real leaders don't need the spotlight.

The most influential moments aren't the ones where everyone sees you leading.

They're the quiet ones.

The behind-the-scenes decisions.

The conversations where you guide without directing.

The times you let someone else take the spotlight because they needed it more than you did.

The ego wants to lead from the front.

Sometimes you lead best from the back, lifting others higher than they could go on their own.

Where could I step back so someone else can step up?

Resolve is contagious.

When things are hard, people don't need someone with all the answers.

They need someone who refuses to fold.

Not false positivity.

But honesty about where things stand.

Steady resolve says there's a way forward, and we'll find it.

Resolve doesn't mean you're fearless.

It means staying committed and keeping moving.

Your resolve becomes a source of strength for everyone around you.

Am I showing resolve or am I folding under pressure?

You were invited for a reason.

"My goal is to be the dumbest person in the room."

I get the spirit of it: stay humble, keep learning, don't let your ego run the meeting.

Nobody pulls up a chair for someone who brings nothing.

How you walk in tells people everything before you open your mouth.

Whether your mindset is to consume or to contribute.

Come ready to learn.

But also walk in looking for where you can contribute.

Leave as someone worth inviting back.

Did I contribute or take up space?

INTEGRITY

People follow what you live.

Lead by example.

You can't demand from others what you're not willing to demonstrate yourself.

My mom didn't talk about hard work.

She lived it, never called in, no complaints, no excuses.

Her example followed me into my IT career.

I loved staying late, coming in early, and working the hard problems.

People don't follow your words.

They follow your behavior.

What standard am I teaching people by the way I lead?

Serve first, influence follows.

The leaders I respect most aren't the ones with the biggest teams.

They're the ones who are there when it's inconvenient, when there's no camera, when nobody's keeping score.

They are not trying to be influential.

They're too busy making a difference.

The moment you stop serving, you stop leading.

No matter what your title says.

People remember who was there for them.

Where am I trying to be impressive instead of useful?

Leadership is balanced, firm, and kind.

Some leaders are strong but rude.

Kind but weak.

Bold but bulldozing.

I've worked for all of them.

The worst were the managers who yelled and belittled everyone around them.

That led to high turnover and a culture nobody wanted to be part of.

The leaders who made an impression were different.

They had high standards and uplifted everyone around them.

But what made them strong was the ability to push without bulldozing.

That kind of balance is a daily decision about who you're choosing to be.

Which side of this balance am I falling off?

Earn it.

Influence is earned daily.

Through consistency.

Through follow-through.

Through being the same person in private that you are in public.

Every time you keep your word, you earn it.

Every time you break it, you lose a little.

The people around you are always watching, not your highlights, but your patterns.

Influence is earned in the ordinary moments, not the spotlight.

Am I earning my influence today or coasting on yesterday?

Build influence that lasts.

What happens when you leave the room?

Do people live up to the standard you set?

Do they hold themselves accountable?

Do they lead themselves better because of the time they spent with you?

Or does everything fall apart the moment you're not there?

If your influence only works when you're watching, it's not influence.

It's supervision.

Real influence leaves a mark that doesn't need your presence to hold.

Does my influence last when I leave the room?

RESPECT

Influence grows where people feel seen and safe.

Lead with your heart, not your head.

Early in my career, I thought I had to have all the right answers.

The more I knew, the more valuable I would be.

But I wasn't connecting with people.

The shift came when I stopped leading with my head and started leading with my heart.

That meant putting people first.

Caring more about where they were than where I wanted them to be.

Listening beyond the words they were sharing.

And doing the right thing, even when it wasn't easy.

Once people feel that, influence flows.

What situation in my life needs less logic and more heart?

Be present, not productive.

There are people in your life who carry more than they show or share.

Emotionally, mentally, physically.

And when they finally open up, the instinct is to fix it or stay silent.

Neither works.

What helps is slowing down and being present.

It takes time, and nothing changes overnight, but eventually people feel the difference.

Who in my life needs my presence more than my answers?

Listen to what's unsaid.

People don't always tell you what's really going on.

But they will always show you.

The body language.

The tone shift.

The thing they almost said but pulled back.

The silence that lasted a beat too long.

I've learned to listen for what's underneath the words.

That's where the real conversation is happening.

Influence requires paying attention to what people can't or won't say out loud.

What is someone in my life trying to tell me without saying it?

Be interested, not impressive.

The leaders who impacted me most weren't the ones with the best credentials.

They were the ones who asked about me.

Who remembered what I was working on.

Who followed up.

That kind of attention is rare, and it's magnetic.

Stop trying to be interesting.

Start being genuinely curious about the people around you.

That's what people remember.

Am I genuinely interested, or am I just trying to impress?

People can tell if they're a transaction.

You can't fake this.

People know when you see them as a transaction rather than as a person.

They feel the difference in how you listen, respond, and give time.

Influence built on genuine care outlasts influence built on charm and deception.

Stephen Covey said it best:
Every interaction is a deposit or a withdrawal.

Do the people in my life feel valued by me or used?

Commitment requires safety.

Create a space where people can be honest, be themselves, and still move forward together.

The moment people feel they have to fall in line, you get compliance, not commitment.

The strongest teams, families, and communities I've seen aren't the ones where everyone thinks the same.

They're the ones where differences are respected, and purpose is shared.

Is it safe to disagree with me?

EMPOWERMENT

Real influence multiplies others.

Delegate to develop.

One of the fastest ways to empower someone is to delegate work that matters.

Not the tasks you don't want.

But the ones that will stretch them.

Challenge people.

Give them work that helps them grow into someone they are not yet.

Who am I holding back by not delegating important work to them?

Empower, don't enable.

A client kept asking me, "What would you do?"

What he really wanted was relief from responsibility.

I refused to answer, not because I didn't know, but because he already did.

Handing him my answer would have felt like help.

It would have made him weaker.

Every time you solve it for someone, you teach them they can't.

Real influence isn't giving people your answers.

It's helping them trust themselves.

Are the people I lead growing, or just growing dependent on me?

Leaders develop leaders.

Early in my career, I felt lucky to have a job and make good money.

I made it a point to go above and beyond.

I would work late, come in early.

Volunteer for work others didn't want to do.

The result?

People stopped trying; they expected me to do all the grunt work.

And when I finally stopped, things started to fall through the cracks.

Not because the work was hard, but because I taught everyone around me that it was my job to handle everything.

That's not leadership; that's hoarding.

Am I building leaders around me or just followers?

Influence draws greatness out of others.

People are more capable than they believe.

Your job isn't to convince them.

It's to create the space where they can prove it to themselves.

In coaching, the breakthroughs rarely come from what I say.

They come from the right question at the right moment.

The permission to think differently.

The space to be honest without judgment.

People don't need you to be great for them.

They need you to believe in them long enough for them to believe in themselves.

What greatness am I drawing out of the people around me?

Control kills influence.

Management controls behavior.

Leadership influences behavior.

When you tell people exactly what to do and how to do it, you're not leading.

You're pushing your way on everyone else.

Real leaders trust people and get out of their way.

I've watched volunteers, clients, and team members exceed every expectation.

Not because I controlled the process, but because I trusted them and let them own the execution.

Micromanagement is about fear.

Fear that they won't do it your way.

Fear that you'll lose control.

Trust is influence.

Am I leading with trust or managing with fear?

S

SELF-AWARENESS

Self-awareness is the ability to focus on yourself and notice if your actions, thoughts, and emotions align with your internal standards.

That's it.

No complicated psychology.

Just the willingness to look honestly at what you're doing and ask: Is this who I want to be?

It's an easy question to avoid.

Not because you don't care, but because the answer might be uncomfortable.

It's easier to stay busy or blame everyone around you than to stop and look at yourself.

But you can't fix what you won't acknowledge.

Self-awareness isn't about being hard on yourself.

It's about being honest with yourself.

Seeing what's really happening without judging it.

The decision:

Tell yourself the truth without judgment so you can choose differently.

AWARENESS

You can't change what you won't face.

Get in the game.

It's easy to think that being busy and having a full calendar means you're in the arena.

Theodore Roosevelt said it best:

"The credit belongs to the man in the arena."

Not the one watching from the sidelines.

Not the one analyzing from a safe distance.

The one who shows up, gets hit, and keeps going.

The hardest part isn't finding time.

It's being honest enough to admit when you're filling time instead of using it.

Am I in the arena or on the sidelines, staying busy?

Awareness changes you.

Awareness doesn't fix everything overnight.

But stay with it long enough and everything changes.

Once you see a pattern, you can't unsee it.

You can choose to ignore it, but it doesn't go away.

Once you name a behavior, it loses its grip.

I still get pulled in.

I still react.

But the difference is I catch it faster now.

The win isn't perfection.

The win is noticing sooner.

What am I finally starting to notice that I couldn't see before?

Your filters shape your reality.

Every situation you walk into, you're filtering through the lens of your own stories, fears, and experiences.

Two people can sit in the same meeting and walk away with completely different versions of what happened.

Your version isn't always the truth.

It's your personal interpretation.

And your interpretation is shaped by everything you're carrying and everything you've been through.

How might my filters be distorting what I'm seeing right now?

Inside shapes outside.

I know I'm stuck when I start replaying the past or worrying about what may never happen.

I have to remind myself that the past is done and the future isn't here yet.

What matters is paying attention to what's happening inside right now.

Your thoughts, your emotional state, and your limiting beliefs are shaping every decision you make.

You can manage everything on the outside and still feel off.

What's happening inside me right now that I haven't stopped to examine?

Tell the truth.

You know the truth before you try to justify it.

You can:

Work harder.

Try new tactics.

Change your environment.

None of it matters if you never face the truth.

You'll keep recreating the problem.

The hard part isn't finding it.

It's being willing to sit with it long enough to do something about it.

That's where clarity begins.

What truth am I avoiding because it would require me to change?

PATTERNS

Your patterns don't lie.

Start with you.

I'm not 100% successful, but when someone's behavior bothers me:

I try to slow down and ask:
Why is this bothering me?

No one has frustrated me more than my son, because he is a mirror reflection of me.

I see my strengths in him, my stubbornness, and my untapped potential.

When he doesn't tap into the resources I know he has, it deeply irritates me.

The frustration is never about him.

It's always about me.

What is my frustration trying to teach me about myself?

Notice the narrative.

We don't react to reality.

We react to the story we tell ourselves about it.

A look becomes disrespect.

Silence becomes rejection.

Feedback becomes a personal attack.

The story is already running.

Separate what happened from what you made it mean.

Am I reacting to what happened or the story I created?

Respond, don't react.

Reacting is automatic.

It's the impulse pulling you before you even realize what happened.

Responding is intentional.

It's feeling the pull and choosing something different.

The reaction is a pattern.

The pause is your chance to break it.

What would change if I paused before my next reaction?

Patterns are feedback.

You can explain away a single moment.

You can justify one bad decision.

But when the same thing keeps happening in different jobs, different relationships, different situations, the patterns are showing you something.

That's not bad luck.

That's data.

Stop arguing with the pattern.

What pattern have I been arguing with instead of learning from?

Turn around.

I spent years looking for better answers.

Someone was always selling the next thing: a new strategy, a new system, a better way.

I figured, what do I have to lose?

I gave it a try.

Then another and another.

I kept thinking something would show me a clear path.

It never did.

What moved the needle was looking inward at what I was feeling, avoiding or repeating.

Clarity doesn't come from more information.

It comes from looking at the patterns you've been too busy to notice.

Am I looking outside for something that can only be found inside?

IDENTITY

Separate who you are from how you're acting.

Know yourself.

Socrates said it first: "Know thyself."

It's still the hardest thing to do.

Knowing yourself means knowing who you are, independent of what others think, expect, or need from you.

I've had times where I was so focused on being what everyone else needed that I lost track of what I needed.

Know yourself first.

Then lead others from a position of strength.

Do I know who I am when nobody needs anything from me?

Identity and Behavior.

Before I started to meditate, I thought:

"I can't slow down."

"I'm not great at being quiet with my thoughts."

I wasn't describing what I did.

I was defining who I was.

I boxed myself in and thought that was who I was.

The shift came when I learned to separate the two.

"I acted impatient" is not the same as
"I am impatient."

Identity is who you are.

Behavior is what you do.

Behavior is adjustable.

Where am I confusing a behavior with my identity?

Feelings don't define you.

There are moments when I feel down.

Plans fall apart and I fall short.

Those moments are real.

So are the feelings.

A thought and a feeling are behaviors.

They move through you.

They are not a verdict on who you are.

Feeling low doesn't make you weak.

It makes you human.

The moment you see it for what it is and not your identity, something shifts.

You're still whole.

You're still capable.

Now choose what you do with it.

Am I treating this feeling as a fact about who I am, or as a moment I'm moving through?

Beliefs steer decisions.

If you believe you're not enough, you'll sabotage opportunities.

If you believe you can't change, you won't try.

Catch the limiting thoughts before they influence your decisions.

You're not stuck because of your circumstances.

You're stuck because of what you believe about them.

What do I believe about my circumstances that isn't true?

Choose who you become.

I've spent a lot of time trying to figure out who I am.

That search never really ends; it evolves.

But somewhere along the way, I stopped waiting for the answer and started paying attention to my choices.

The decisions I make under pressure.

The way I respond when things don't go my way.

The habits I keep when no one is watching.

You don't discover yourself.

You decide who you are.

Every day.

Who am I becoming based on the choices I'm making right now?

Truth before action.

There is always a gap between who you know you are and how you've been acting.

When you see it, you have two choices.

Ignore it, justify it, blame something external.

Or acknowledge it and move forward.

One honest step is all it takes.

Truth without action is just awareness.

Am I the kind of person who faces the truth or finds reason to avoid it?

OWNERSHIP

Awareness becomes change when you own it.

Honesty beats self-attack.

Awareness without acceptance turns into shame.

You can't shame yourself into growth.

On occasion, I still think "I should be past this by now."

The problem is repeating the story, allowing it to soak into your being, and doing nothing.

See it clearly.

Own it.

Then do something about it.

That's ownership without shame.

Can I own what I see without using it against myself?

Growth requires openness.

Ownership requires vulnerability.

You have to be willing to say:

"I was wrong."

"I don't know."

"I need help."

For a long time, I wore self-reliance like armor.

Asking for help felt like the ultimate weakness.

But the moments that changed me most were the ones where I let my guard down.

Vulnerability and openness aren't weaknesses.

What am I protecting by hiding behind strength?

Justify less.

There's a difference between justifying something that happened and owning it.

Justifying what happened protects your ego and avoids responsibility.

Ownership acknowledges your role, learns from it, and moves forward.

I've caught myself justifying situations I should have owned.

For example, a failed goal:

I'd say, "I've been too busy."

When the truth was that I didn't make it a priority.

The more I justified it, the less I changed and the worse I felt.

The moment I stopped justifying and started taking ownership, I was able to move forward.

Where am I justifying when I should be owning?

The real work is internal.

Most of my growth didn't come from huge external changes.

It came from small internal shifts.

Taking ownership instead of repeating the same old patterns.

Admitting I was wrong without making it mean I was broken.

The outer world changes when the inner world shifts.

Every change that mattered began with one honest look inward.

What inner shift have I been avoiding that could change everything?

Knowing isn't doing.

I've had moments where I knew something had to change.

I thought about it, talked about it, journaled about it, but didn't do anything.

Awareness without ownership just kept me in the same loop.

The moment I stopped thinking about it, owned it, and did something, things started to shift.

What am I aware of but refuse to own?

Feedback is the mirror.

One of the fastest ways to personal growth is through feedback from others.

But feedback and validation are two different things.

Those closest to you see what you can't or won't.

They notice the patterns that you have normalized.

The blind spots that you've learned to live with.

That kind of feedback is priceless.

Even when it's uncomfortable to receive.

Your circle is your best source of feedback.

Who in my life is trying to give me feedback that I need to own?

E

ENERGY

Energy is the fuel behind every other decision in R.I.S.E.

It operates on two levels.

Physical energy is your capacity: sleep, nutrition, movement, and recovery.

Internal energy is how you feel and how you carry yourself.

Physical energy is the tank.

Internal energy is what you do with it.

That's not only sleep and working out.

It's what you say yes to, who you spend time with, and if the work means anything to you.

All of it fills the tank or drains it.

The difference is whether you're managing your state or letting your state manage you.

State management is the ability to select and shift your internal state, focus, and choices.

Run low, and everything else gets harder.

You think slower, react faster, and settle for less than you're capable of.

Energy is the decision that sustains all the others.

———— ✦ ————

The decision:

Protect what fuels you. Energy spent in the wrong places leaves nothing for the right ones.

FUEL

You can't perform on empty.

Energy decides.

You can have the right strategy, the right skills, and the right intentions.

None of it matters if you're running on empty.

Energy shapes how you think, how you respond, and how you lead.

When energy is high, obstacles feel manageable.

When energy is low, even simple tasks feel heavy.

You can't think straight or lead with confidence when you're depleted.

Energy is the deciding factor.

How is my energy affecting my decisions right now?

Take your MEDS.

Physical energy gets treated like a reward.

Something you'll get to after the deadline, after the project, when things slow down.

Things never slow down.

Your body isn't waiting for your schedule to clear.

You can't outwork a depleted body.

You can't out-think exhaustion.

Brendon Burchard calls it MEDS:

Meditation. Exercise. Diet. Sleep.

Skip one, and you feel it.

Skip two, and everything gets harder.

Skip all four, and you'll wonder why nothing is working.

Which of the four am I skipping, and what is it costing me?

Two tanks.

Physical energy gives you capacity.

But internal energy, how you feel about what's happening in your life, is the multiplier.

You can have a full tank physically and still be running on empty inside.

Unresolved stress.

Emotional weight you're carrying.

Work that feels meaningless.

These drain your internal fuel faster than a missed workout.

You can't perform on empty physically or emotionally.

Both tanks need fuel.

What's draining my internal fuel right now?

Fatigue lowers standards.

When you're depleted, everything looks harder than it is.

The conversation you'd normally handle gets avoided.

The decision that takes five minutes gets put off for weeks.

You don't drop the bar on purpose.

You're just too tired to reach it.

Rested, you handle it.

You say what needs to be said, decide, and move on.

The standard didn't move.

You finally had the energy to meet it.

Keep your tank full, and the bar stays where you set it.

What standard am I letting slide because I'm too tired to maintain it?

Reset before you break.

Recovery isn't just sleep.

It's mental off-ramps.

Time when you're not producing, fixing, or proving anything.

Waiting until you're burned out to address your energy is a mistake.

By then, recovery takes at least twice as long.

The best time to protect your energy is when things are going well.

Build the habits before the breakdown, not after.

Rest isn't something you earn.

It's something you owe to yourself.

Do I rest with purpose, or only when I crash?

STATE

Your state is something you manage.
Not something you wait for.

Change your state.

Your state isn't something that happens to you.

It's something you create.

There will be moments when you can't change the circumstances.

In those moments, your state is the only thing you can control.

Stand up.

Walk.

Change your breathing.

Change your focus.

Your body leads your mind more than your mind leads your body.

Act first.

The energy follows.

Am I waiting to feel ready, or am I choosing to act?

Your inner voice matters.

Negative self-talk is one of the quietest energy drains.

It sounds reasonable:

"This is just how I am."

"I should be further along by now."

"What's the point?"

It doesn't feel like a drain.

It passes as honesty.

But your body absorbs every word.

The internal dialogue is either recharging you or depleting you.

There's no neutral.

How is my internal dialogue recharging or depleting me?

Negativity drains.

Your internal state is a choice.

Not always an easy one, but always yours.

You can think about the worst-case scenario.

Or you can redirect your focus to what you can control.

Overthinking the negative what-ifs drains.

It feels productive.

It's not.

It's energy leaking through a thousand small thoughts that don't move anything forward.

Where is my mental energy going that isn't moving anything forward?

Your race, your pace.

Every minute you spend measuring yourself against someone else's best moments is a minute you're not investing in yourself.

I've wasted more time than I'd like to admit comparing my progress against other people.

Protect your state from the trap of measuring your mile 3 against someone else's mile 20.

Whose pace am I measuring myself against?

Set the tone.

If you're a parent, a leader, a coach, or a partner, your energy sets the room before you do.

Burned-out energy doesn't stay confined.

It leaks into your tone, your patience, your decisions.

The people closest to you absorb what you're carrying, whether you intend it or not.

Protecting your energy isn't selfish.

It's responsible.

The people who depend on you need you full, not empty.

Who is paying the price for my low energy right now?

BOUNDARIES

Protect what fuels you.

Filters, not walls.

Saying yes when you mean no.

Over-explaining.

Letting others' urgency dictate your pace.

Boundaries aren't walls.

They're energy filters.

Without them, other people's priorities consume yours.

I had to learn to say:

"No."

"That's not for me right now."

"I don't have the capacity to do this."

What boundary do I need to set to protect my energy this week?

Every yes has a price.

Every commitment draws from the same place.

I used to say yes to everything because I felt like I had to.

I was saying yes out of obligation when I could have said no.

The cost was resentment, exhaustion, and diluted impact.

Protecting your energy means being honest about what deserves your best and letting go of what doesn't.

What do I need to say no to so I can fully say yes to what matters?

Relationships matter.

Some relationships restore you.

Some drain you.

Pay attention to how you feel afterward.

The relationships that matter are the ones where you feel seen without having to perform, challenged without being torn down, and restored simply by being present.

Protect them.

Invest in them.

If they don't, create space and strong boundaries.

Which relationships are restoring me, and which need space?

Recovery routine.

Recovery isn't a single vacation or a great workout.

It's the daily routine.

What time you go to sleep.

Whether you move your body.

How you start your morning.

Small deposits add up.

These small daily decisions are the difference between running and dragging.

Energy isn't fixed by one big choice.

It's built by the small ones you make every day.

Build a sustainable routine.

What daily routine would help me recover before I need rescue?

ALIGNMENT

Misalignment drains.
Meaning renews.

Alignment.

Same workload.

Same responsibilities.

Completely different experiences depending on what the work means to you.

I've had the calendar full and felt alive.

I've had the calendar light and felt crushed.

The difference was whether the work was aligned with what mattered to me.

Pushing harder on meaningless work just depletes you faster.

Meaning doesn't always find you.

Sometimes you have to go look for it.

And sometimes the most energizing thing you can do isn't adding something new.

It's releasing something old.

Where am I out of alignment with who I am?

Celebrate the win.

I've always struggled with celebrating wins.

My go-to was to finish one thing and move on to the next.

What I learned is that pausing to acknowledge a win is worth it.

I don't celebrate every win every time.

But the ones that matter deserve a moment, even if it's just saying, "I did that."

You worked for it.

Let yourself feel it.

When was the last time I paused and enjoyed a win?

Purpose.

Early in my IT career, I was good at the work, and the money was great.

I was always looking for the next problem to fix and the next paycheck.

I was successful by most measures and empty by the ones that mattered.

Purpose isn't what you do.

It's why you do it.

Your real purpose always points beyond yourself.

When the why is missing, even great work leaves you hollow.

When it's present, even hard work feels meaningful.

Find the why, and everything changes.

What is the deeper why behind the work I'm doing now?

Mission.

Early in my coaching and speaking career, I talked at people.

I provided great information.

I gave them all the answers.

It felt like teaching, but there was something missing.

The shift came when I started to facilitate.

Real conversations emerged; people shared and taught each other.

That's when I realized my mission wasn't to have all the answers.

It was to create a space where people could find their own answers.

Mission is what you do to live out your purpose.

When your actions align with your mission, the work has direction and meaning.

Are my daily actions aligned with my mission?

SELF-ACCOUNTABILITY

Self-accountability is not a separate pillar.

It runs through every decision in R.I.S.E.

Resourcefulness without accountability is just good intentions.

Influence without accountability is performance.

Self-awareness without accountability is overthinking.

Energy without accountability is grind with no direction.

Without self-accountability, the other four decisions are just ideas.

They sound good.

They might even feel right.

But knowing the right answer and living it are two different things.

The missing piece isn't more information.

It's self-accountability.

It doesn't become real until you own it, daily, privately, without anyone checking in on you.

— ✦ —

The decision:

Own your choices, your standards, and your results without blaming, excusing, or avoiding.

ACCOUNTABILITY

What you own, you can change.

Keep your word.

There was a time when I thought accountability was all about discipline.

I thrived on pushing harder, doing more, and being tough on myself.

But pushing harder isn't the same as keeping your word to yourself.

Every time you keep a commitment to yourself, you're telling yourself you matter.

And when you break those commitments, you're doing the opposite.

Am I worth keeping my word to myself?

Build self-accountability, not dependency.

Accountability groups and partners can be valuable; a great one can change your life.

A great accountability partner helps you build self-accountability.

A bad one becomes a crutch; someone you can blame for not doing what you were supposed to do.

"They didn't hold me accountable."

That sentence is the problem.

Nobody else should be holding you accountable.

That's your job.

Where have I been blaming others when the standard is mine to keep?

Move past blame.

You can blame your upbringing.

Your circumstances.

The economy, your boss, or your partner.

Blame keeps you in the past.

Accountability moves you forward.

"This is what happened."

"This is my part in it."

"This is what I'm going to do next."

Just facts and forward motion.

What would I do differently if I stopped blaming and started acting?

Own the choice, own the consequence.

Every choice has a consequence.

Including the choice to do nothing.

Self-accountability means owning the choice and what it produced.

You didn't end up here by accident.

And you won't get out by accident either.

Your life is the result of the choices you've made.

So is the life you want.

What consequence am I living with right now because of a choice I made?

Wait for no one.

Nobody is coming to save you.

Nobody is going to do the work for you.

The sooner you accept that, the sooner things start to change.

This isn't punishment.

It's freedom.

Stop waiting for someone else to hold you to a standard and start holding yourself to one.

What am I waiting for someone else to do that I should be doing myself?

CONVICTION

Who are you when no one's watching?

Do it when it's hard.

Anyone can be anything when there's an audience.

But who are you when there's no audience, no one checking in on you?

Are you able to do the things you need to do without someone talking you into it?

If the answer is no, that's not a character flaw.

It's a skill you haven't built YET.

Can I hold myself to a high standard without anyone forcing me?

Private wins.

Social media makes it easy to perform accountability.

Post the workout.

Share the early morning.

Show the world you're doing the work.

Posting can help create a commitment and keep you honest.

Looking accountable and being accountable are two different things.

Self-accountability isn't a public performance.

It's a private standard.

Who you are alone is the person you really are.

When the audience is gone, is the standard still there?

Do it anyway.

Writing this book was a hard commitment to keep.

After a few drafts, the excuses came flooding.

There were weeks I didn't want to open the document.

It was draining and easy to put off.
The internal negotiation was real: tomorrow, next week, when I'm inspired.

That's the negotiation conviction has to win.

You don't have to feel like it.

You just have to do it anyway.

What excuses keep winning?

It's in the details.

The small things reveal the big things.

How you handle the boring tasks.

How you treat people who can't do anything for you.

Whether you clean up after yourself when nobody's looking.

It's all in the details.

If you cut corners on the small stuff, you'll cut corners on the big stuff.

It's the same muscle.

Where am I cutting corners that I think don't matter?

FOLLOW-THROUGH

Close the gap between words and behavior.

Behavior never lies.

Words are easy.

Behavior is the truth.

Your actions already told the story.

Every time you say one thing and do another, you teach yourself that your word doesn't matter.

Keeping your word to yourself sounds straightforward.

It's not.

Every time you honor a commitment, you build self-trust.

Every time you don't, you chip away at it.

Winning doesn't live in the big moments.

It lives in the small daily ones.

That's how you turn "I want to" into "I did."

What do my actions say that my words do not?

Drop the excuses.

I still fall into this trap.

When I don't follow through on something I committed to, the first instinct is to explain why.

The excuses make me feel better in the moment.

But they don't change what I didn't do.

Excuses protect your ego.

They keep you safe and stuck at the same time.

Stop explaining and start doing.

Move forward.

Which excuse do I refuse to let go?

Ask.

For a long time, I needed things but wouldn't ask.

I figured it out myself or went without.

All to avoid asking someone for something.

I told myself it was about not wanting to seem weak or vulnerable.

But the truth was, I was scared to hear no.

A no felt like rejection.

So, I stayed silent and called it self-sufficiency.

I still have to remind myself sometimes.

But I'm significantly better.

The only thing worse than hearing no is never asking at all.

Because a no is better than not knowing.

What am I not asking for because I'm afraid of the answer?

Stop looking for hacks.

We live in a world that sells magical instant results.

And we buy into it because we want it to be true.

It doesn't exist.

Never has.

Never will.

Do the work.

No app.

No system.

No guru is going to do it for you.

Am I looking for a shortcut when I already know what needs to be done?

PRIORITIES

Stop delaying.
Start deciding.

Avoidance becomes debt.

Avoidance feels like relief.

It's really debt.

Every hard conversation you postpone, every decision you delay, every standard you let slide. It's all waiting for you.

And the interest compounds.

Address issues when they're small instead of waiting until they're a crisis.

The discomfort of now is always cheaper than the consequences later.

What am I avoiding today that will cost me more tomorrow?

Bad habits can become heavy.

Success is shaped by the small decisions that don't feel important.

The workout you keep putting off.

The boundary that keeps sliding.

The habit you keep pushing to next week.

Each one is light.

Barely noticeable.

Until one day you wake up and realize you're carrying a heavy weight you built yourself.

Catch it, make it a priority, and address it while it's still light.

Where am I letting something slide that's slowly getting heavier?

Your calendar reveals your real priorities.

I don't have time is the #1 excuse I hear.

And it's almost never true.

You have time for what you prioritize.

The question is whether you're being honest about your priorities.

Look at where your time goes, not where you say it goes, and own it.

If someone looked at how I spend my time, what would they say my real priorities are?

Results over comfort.

There is a difference between being comfortable in life and being comfortable on your couch.

A cozy blanket restores you.

Getting comfortable in life drains you.

Staying in the wrong situations, avoiding the hard conversation, tolerating what you said you wouldn't, none of that is rest.

It's avoidance.

You're not saving energy by waiting.

You're spending it.

Every day you delay acting on a decision you've already made, you pay for it.

Am I confusing comfort with rest?

Start now.

You can't go back and undo the past.

Don't beat yourself up for what you didn't do yesterday.

Decide what you're going to do today.

Stop looking back.

Start looking forward.

What you choose today creates your tomorrow.

What decision have I been putting off that I need to make today?

This is where it starts.

You've read the reflections.

You've sat with the questions.

Now comes the part that matters.

R.I.S.E. isn't something you finish.

It's something you practice every day.

One decision at a time.

Resourcefulness when it's easier to wait.

Influence when it's easier to withdraw.

Self-awareness when it's easier to avoid.

Energy when it's easier to burn out.

You don't have to get it right all the time.

You just have to keep deciding.

That's the practice.

That's the rise.

That's who I'm choosing to become.

Now it's your time to R.I.S.E.

~ Ricardo

ABOUT THE AUTHOR

Ricardo León is an executive coach, speaker, trainer, and author helping leaders think clearly and perform differently.

His journey began in a small East Texas town, where he was raised by a determined single mother who taught him that grit and vision can outpace circumstance.

Those lessons fueled a twenty-five-year career as a Unix Systems Engineer in Fortune 500 companies.

Since 2015, he has been coaching, training, and leading Circle of Success, a mastermind community for leaders ready to rise.

In 2017, Ricardo co-founded Baskets For Good, a nonprofit Thanksgiving initiative serving families across North Texas. As of 2025, it has provided 302,476 meals to more than 5,000 families. Learn more at basketsforgood.org

Ricardo holds a B.S. in Psychology and advanced certifications in Neuro-Linguistic Programming and High-Performance Coaching.

SIMPLE BY DESIGN

One reflection. One question. One decision.

That was intentional.

R.I.S.E. is not complicated.

The framework exists to give you a clear, repeatable way to check in with yourself daily without overthinking it.

If something on these pages stopped you, challenged you, or gave you language for something you'd already been feeling, that's the work.

MORE TO COME

Book 2 goes beneath the surface.

It explores the why behind each pillar, the patterns that keep capable people stuck, the decisions that change behavior, and the tools to close the gap between who you are and who you're committed to being.

Same framework. Deeper work.

ricardoleon.net

www.ingramcontent.com/pod-product-compliance
Lightning Source LLC
LaVergne TN
LVHW090522110826
845146LV00003B/952

* 9 7 9 8 9 9 5 0 4 3 1 0 2 *